Learning Volleyball

This book was given to me by:

_____

*Here you can put
a photo of yourself.*

My name: _____

My birthday: _____

My address: _____

_____

LEARNING VOLLEYBALL

**Katrin Barth &
Richard Heuchert**

Sports Science Consultant:
Dr. Berndt Barth

Meyer & Meyer Sport

Original Title: *Ich lerne Volleyball*
© Aachen: Meyer & Meyer, 2005
Translated by Petra Haynes
AAA Translation, St. Louis, Missouri, USA
www.AAATranslation.com

British Library Cataloguing in Publication Data
A catalogue record for this book is available from the British Library

Learning Volleyball
Katrin Barth / Richard Heuchert
Oxford: Meyer & Meyer Sport (UK) Ltd., 2007
ISBN-10: 1-84126-197-1
ISBN-13: 978-1-84126-197-3

© 2007 by Meyer & Meyer Sport (UK) Ltd.
Aachen, Adelaide, Auckland, Budapest, Graz, Johannesburg,
New York, Olten (CH), Oxford, Singapore, Toronto
Member of the World
Sports Publishers' Association (WSPA)
www.w-s-p-a.org
Printed and bound by: B.O.S.S Druck und Medien GmbH, Germany
ISBN-10: 1-84126-197-1
ISBN-13: 978-1-84126-197-3
E-Mail: verlag@m-m-sports.com

TABLE OF CONTENTS

Please note:
The exercises and practical suggestions in this book have been carefully chosen and reviewed by the authors. However, the authors are not liable for accidents or damages of any kind incurred in connection with the content of this book.

HI THERE, DEAR VOLLEYBALL BEGINNER!
I AM FELIX THE CAT, AND I KNOW LOTS ABOUT VOLLEYBALL.
I CAN RUN, JUMP AND DIVE LIKE NO OTHER.

IN THIS BOOK YOU WILL FIND OUT LOTS ABOUT THE GAME OF
VOLLEYBALL AND I WILL ALWAYS BE THERE WITH YOU.
I THINK WE'LL HAVE LOTS OF FUN TOGETHER.

YOU WILL OFTEN SEE PICTURES OF FELIX THE CAT IN THE BOOK.

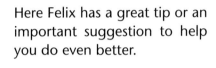

Here Felix has a great tip or an important suggestion to help you do even better.

Pretty tough! Sometimes Felix has a task or a riddle for you. You will find these tasks next to the question mark.

The answers and solutions are at the end of the book.

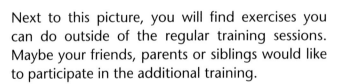

Next to this picture, you will find exercises you can do outside of the regular training sessions. Maybe your friends, parents or siblings would like to participate in the additional training.

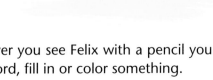

Whenever you see Felix with a pencil you can record, fill in or color something.

You can use this volleyball book like a diary. Record your progress and goals.

When you have become an experienced player you can enjoy reading about how it all began. If you like, you can add photos of yourself and your team or collect signatures.

You will find a "blank" volleyball next to some important techniques and special exercises. Once you have mastered the technique pretty well or you have completed the suggested exercise, you can reward yourself by coloring the volleyball with your favorite colors. If you like you can try it out right now on the first ball!

We are the funny yellow practice guys, and we'll show you how to do an exercise by yourself or with friends.

If you have tried something new, you can color the blank ball.

I am the little blue mistake guy. I deliberately make mistakes – only to help you, of course! Let's see if you can recognize them all. If you're not sure, check the solution pages.

Felix loves ball games but he just can't choose one of the many ball sports. Which ball sports do you recognize in this picture?

Do you know any more ball sports? Write them down here!

_____

_____

........1 DEAR BEGINNING VOLLEYBALL PLAYER

Are you one of those ball-crazy kids who cannot come across a ball without wanting to play with it? Something itches in your fingers and you immediately want to kick the ball or pick it up, throw it, catch it and bounce it.

Sometimes it is a little bouncy super ball, a brightly colored rubber ball or a big, light inflatable ball. It's just plain fun.

But it is even more fun when there are other kids around, and you can pass the ball back and forth, make up games and rules, and fight for victory.

Is that how you became interested in volleyball? Or did the excitement rub off on you from your friends? Maybe you got the idea to learn to play volleyball from watching volleyball games on television. In any case, you have chosen a great sport that is very popular all around the world.

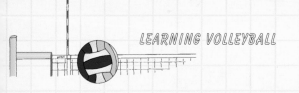

Here are some of the reasons kids like to play volleyball. Which ones apply to you? Check "Yes" or "No"!

	Yes	No
I enjoy sports and romping around.	☐	☐
I enjoy being with other kids.	☐	☐
I want to play on a team.	☐	☐
I'm already very involved in sports.	☐	☐
I am tall.	☐	☐
I have a good feel for the ball.	☐	☐
I can jump high.	☐	☐
I enjoy watching volleyball.	☐	☐
My friends can also play volleyball.	☐	☐
I want to be better than others.	☐	☐
I want to be one of the best in the nation.	☐	☐
I want to become a professional athlete.	☐	☐

If most of your answers are yes, you have chosen the right sport for you.

Many girls and boys learn to play volleyball in a club. They practice regularly, are on teams, and compete against other teams. But you don't necessarily have to become a member of a club to play volleyball. All you need are a ball, a net or just a cord strung up, an open area or the beach, and a few friends and you're ready to go!

In this volleyball book, we have listed some things of interest about your favorite sport. We explain the most important techniques, how to practice them and which mistakes to avoid. You will get numerous

suggestions for practicing alone or with friends. There are also many game ideas to try out. Of course Mom, Dad, your grandparents, siblings and anyone who – like you – enjoys it, is invited to practice.

Some day you may be a super-successful player at the national level or the top player on a successful team. But even if volleyball remains a recreational sport in the gym or on the beach, you will notice how much you get out of this sport. You will learn to play together with others, to become part of a team and to assert yourself. You will learn to fight and have willpower. You won't always be the glorious winner. You will also learn to cope with defeat, botched set points, incorrect passing or bad receiving.

And soon you will notice that playing volleyball regularly has made you better, more persistent, athletic and stronger, and keeps your body fit and healthy.

Whom do you most like to play volleyball with? List their names here or collect their signatures.

This little book is intended to be your companion as you learn to play volleyball. If we ever view something differently from the way your coach, trainer or an experienced player explains it, it doesn't necessarily mean that it is wrong. Just ask questions. Even in volleyball opinions sometimes differ.

When we refer to trainers, coaches, volleyball players, players, referees, etc., we of course are not just talking about men and boys, but also about all women and girls.

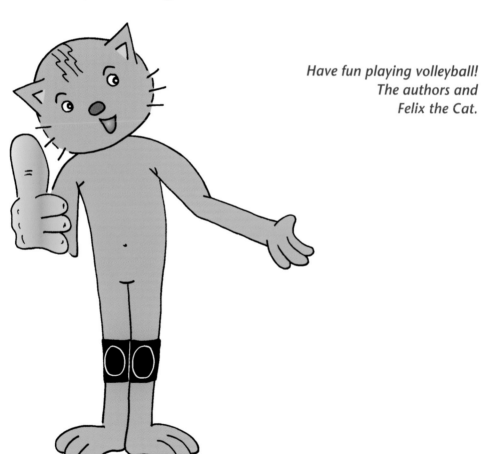

Have fun playing volleyball!
The authors and
Felix the Cat.

Here you can paste a nice photo of yourself playing volleyball.

. . . . 2 HOW VOLLEYBALL BEGAN

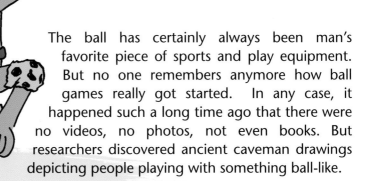

The ball has certainly always been man's favorite piece of sports and play equipment. But no one remembers anymore how ball games really got started. In any case, it happened such a long time ago that there were no videos, no photos, not even books. But researchers discovered ancient caveman drawings depicting people playing with something ball-like.

There were the silly games in which the ball was played with the hand, the head or the foot. Stone age people used sticks as bats, and the Native Americans even had a game in which the players received and played the ball with their rear ends.

Many different sports have evolved from the wild ball games of primitive times. You have already identified and recorded a number of these on page 10.

DID YOU KNOW...

...THAT WILLIAM C. MORGAN
FROM MASSACHUSETTS CREATED THE GAME
OF VOLLEYBALL?
THAT WAS IN 1895, MORE THAN 100 YEARS AGO.

...THAT THIS NOVEL GAME
WAS FIRST CALLED "MINTONETTE"?
ONE YEAR LATER THE NAME
WAS CHANGED TO "VOLLEYBALL."

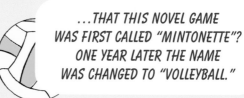

...THAT IN THE FIRST SET OF RULES MORGAN
SPECIFIED A NET HEIGHT OF 6'5"?
THE GAME WAS PLAYED WITH ANY NUMBER OF
PLAYERS IN NINE ROUNDS WITH THREE SERVES FOR
EACH TEAM DURING EACH ROUND.

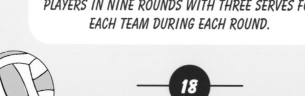

...THAT VOLLEYBALL WAS PART OF THE
MILITARY TRAINING FOR U.S. SOLDIERS AT THE
BEGINNING OF LAST CENTURY?
DURING WORLD WAR I, THEY BROUGHT NETS AND
BALLS TO THEIR BASES, THUS INTRODUCING
VOLLEYBALL TO EUROPE.

...THAT BEACH VOLLEYBALL WAS ALREADY PLAYED 70 YEARS
AGO BY SURFERS IN CALIFORNIA?
SURFERS SOMETIMES HAD TO WAIT A RATHER LONG TIME FOR
THE RIGHT WIND AND A GOOD WAVE,
SO THEY KILLED TIME BY THROWING A FOOTBALL OR BASEBALL.
SOON THIS EVOLVED INTO A GAME WITH RULES.

...THAT VOLLEYBALL ONLY BECAME WELL-KNOWN
AND POPULAR IN GERMANY IN THE 1950S?
TODAY THERE ARE MORE THAN 5,000 CLUBS WITH
MORE THAN HALF A MILLION MEMBERS.

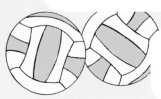

...THAT INDOOR AND BEACH VOLLEYBALL
TODAY RANK AMONG THE MOST POPULAR
SPORTS IN THE WORLD?

How many yellow and white balls are hidden on these two
pages? Before you start to count, look away and guess a
number!

Write the number you guessed in this box:

Write the actual number in this box:

VOLLEYBALL IS A TEAM SPORT

In volleyball two teams always want to compete against each other, score points, and win. Regular teams are formed, clubs are established, and championships are held.

What is the name of your club?

_____

Here you can paste or draw your club's logo.

The team bonds during training and while practicing together.

NATIONAL ASSOCIATIONS

Write down the name of the national volleyball association in your country:

_____

_____

Put the logo of your volleyball association here:

The Elite

Each country has a national indoor volleyball league and rankings for beach volleyball.

Use the charts on the following page to record the names of the current champions or top ranking players. Write the year in the left column and the team in the right column. Start with the current year.

Year	Men's national indoor champion

Year	Women's national indoor champion

Year	Men's beach volleyball rankings

Year	Women's beach volleyball rankings

If you cannot find something look in a trade magazine, check the Internet, or ask your coach.

PICTOGRAM

Surely you have seen different sports depicted as drawings or symbols on television, in the newspaper, on stickers or posters. These symbols are called pictograms. The drawing is very simple, yet everyone immediately recognizes the correct sport. Artists constantly create new symbols for big competitions and events.

Here you can see such a pictogram for volleyball.

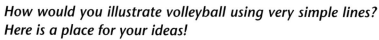

How would you illustrate volleyball using very simple lines? Here is a place for your ideas!

Felix plays volleyball against his mirror image.
But 10 differences have crept into the left "Felix."

Can you find them?

. . . . .3 HI THERE, JÖRG AHMANN!

Jörg Ahmann
Born February 12, 1966
in Grevenbroich, Germany
6"2", 189 lbs.
Electrical engineer
Bronze medal in beach volleyball
at the 2000 Olympics in Sydney

Hi, Jörg! What do you think is so great about volleyball?

Volleyball is just plain fun and can be played almost anywhere with any number of players. You can give great performances as an individual player, but you are also always part of a team.

How did you get started in volleyball?

Physical education in school got me started in volleyball. My teacher often played volleyball with us, and I liked it right away. Of course, I was always a soccer enthusiast as well, but I finally chose volleyball.

What skills does a good volleyball player need?

A volleyball player needs good technique, power, flexibility, endurance, and especially brains. But all the talent in the world is useless without diligent training. Success only comes through lots and lots of practice, even if it isn't much fun on some days.

Do you sometimes not feel like training, too? What do you do then?

Just like anyone else I, too, sometimes want to be lazy and don't feel much like training. I think that happens to everyone. That's when you have to buck up and train anyway. I want to be successful and I don't want to disappoint my training partner. Besides, I still have many goals. I can't fall behind in my training.

You chose beach volleyball. What is so great about that?

I find it fascinating that here every player has to be able to do everything. There are only two players on the court, so you're always on the ball. Besides, I like playing outdoors, in nature. The player always has to readjust to the weather, the sand, the wind, and the sun.

What has been your biggest success?

It took a lot of perseverance and doggedness to become a top beach volleyball player in Germany. It is precisely for that reason that I was overjoyed to win a bronze medal along with my partner Axel Hager, at the 2000 Olympics in Sydney, Australia.

What does volleyball mean to you?

Participating in sports is important and healthy for everyone. Volleyball has made me strong and taught me about camaraderie. But the sport isn't all there is in life. That is why I never neglected school and learned a profession. You cannot be active in competitive sports all your life. That is why a good professional education is important for the future. In the meantime, I have even gotten certified as a professional trainer and would like to pass on my knowledge to young athletes.

Volleyball is probably your favorite hobby. But do you have any other interests?

It is obvious that anyone who wants to be successful has to practice a lot! But spending time with my wife and daughter, both of whom also play beach volleyball, is very important to me. Aside from that, I am interested in computers and many other sports.

What tip would you give young athletes?

If you want to be good and successful, keep at it and don't give up right away if it gets a little difficult. Sometimes it can take a little longer to become successful.

*Thank you very much for the interview
and good luck in the future.*

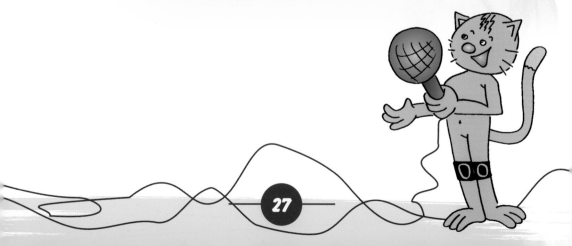

27

MY FAVORITE MALE OR FEMALE PLAYER

Name:

Here you can write down everything you know about your favorite player:
   Birth date, place of residence, hobbies, successes, and much more. You can paste a photo or an autograph.

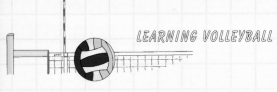

MY FAVORITE CLUB

_____

Logo

Club colors: _____

The best players:
....
....

The biggest wins:
....
....

Here you can collect autographs.

Here is a place for photos.

HAVE YOU HAD A LAUGH TODAY?

THE TRAINER OF A VOLLEYBALL TEAM RUSHES UP TO THE TELEVISION REPORTER AND SAYS WITH AGITATION: "PLEASE, SPEAK A LITTLE SLOWER. MY PLAYERS CANNOT KEEP UP WITH YOUR COMMENTARY!"

PAUL WATCHES MAX PLAY ON THE VOLLEYBALL COURT. THEN HE SAYS, "I GUESS YOU LIKE VOLLEYBALL!" "SURE!" SAYS MAX. "WELL, THEN WHY DON'T YOU LEARN HOW TO PLAY?"

THE TRAINER ASKS TINA: "WHY DO YOU COME TO PRACTICE WITH DIRTY HANDS?" TINA ANSWERS: "I DON'T HAVE ANY OTHER ONES."

ANDY GETS OUT OF THE SHOWER AFTER TRAINING. THE COACH ASKS WITH CONCERN: "BOY, YOU'RE SO PALE. ARE YOU NOT FEELING WELL?" "OH, IT'S NOTHING. I JUST WASHED MYSELF TOO THOROUGHLY."

"WELL, ANNE, HOW WAS YOUR PRACTICE TODAY," ASKS FATHER. "GREAT!" ANSWERS ANNE. "I MUST HAVE BEEN REALLY GOOD BECAUSE THE COACH HAD TEARS IN HER EYES!'

. . . . 4 NO PAIN, NO GAIN

Maybe you have dreamed about what it would be like to be the best. Everyone cheers you on, is in awe and admires you. The most successful clubs want you on their team. The fans mob you and want your autograph. You are tops in offense, blocks, and hardly an opponent can match your spike.

You are indispensable to your team. For that, you accept congratulations from your teammates, your coach, your fans, your friends and parents …!

But stop! Lying in the grass dreaming of success isn't enough!

If you want to be a good volleyball player, maybe even better than the others, you have to practice often and diligently. That's not always easy and isn't always fun right away.

Diligence leads to success!

GOALS

When you begin to play volleyball you must ask yourself the following questions:

 What is my goal?

 What can I do to reach my goal?

 How can I reach my goal?

What is my goal? Why am I practicing so much?

Just volleying the ball back and forth and playing over the net is fun. But soon you'll probably wish you could receive the ball more confidently or play it back with more precision and cunning. Your friends should pick you for their team because you play so well and reliably. Maybe you finally want to play on a good club team or move up to a higher level as a starter. What would it be like to be discovered by a national trainer and play professionally for a top club? Of course you are still much too young for that right now. Nevertheless, you should already envision bigger goals now. You have to know what you want. If you don't have a goal, practicing soon won't be fun anymore. As you learn more, continue to set bigger goals. That's how the successful players did it, too.

Why do you want to learn to play volleyball? List your goals here!

2 What can I do to reach my goal?

Now you will ask what you can do to improve your performance. Definitely play lots and lots of volleyball. But you also need to do necessary exercises for getting a feel for the ball, technique training, as well as endurance and strength training the coach will do with you. You will have lots of fun with it, but sometimes also not quite as much as other days. Some things seem boring and much too strenuous. But you always have to remember that these exercises help you to reach your goal. Surely you will soon see the progress and you'll notice yourself getting better all the time.

3 How can I reach my goal?

How are things going now that you are improving all the time from practicing? As long as the exercises are easy and relaxed, the muscles only do what they can already do anyway. Only when the exercises become a little strenuous and aren't as easy for you to complete are the muscles being strengthened. So you must exert and strain yourself, and repeat the exercises many times in order to make progress. If you haven't been to volleyball practice for a while you will notice that you have gotten a little worse and get winded more easily. Now it's time to catch up!

So, the more diligently and the more often you practice, the better you will become.

What should a good volleyball player be able to do? Cross out anything that isn't very important. Add anything we may have forgotten!

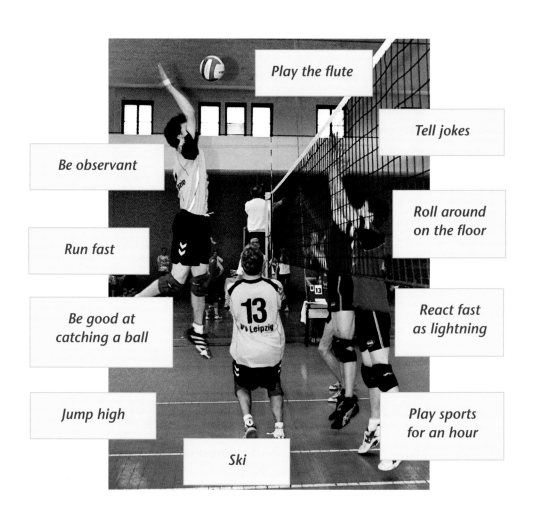

Play the flute

Tell jokes

Be observant

Roll around on the floor

Run fast

Be good at catching a ball

React fast as lightning

Jump high

Play sports for an hour

Ski

PHYSICAL FITNESS IS IMPORTANT

Oh dear, what's wrong with Lucy? After just one hour of volleyball with Felix she is so wiped out that she can barely stand up. She is exhausted and can't play anymore.

Has that ever happened to you? Do you get out of breath easily and lose your strength quickly? Then you need to do something to improve your fitness level!

Most players enjoy competitive games during practice.

What is physical fitness?

When playing volleyball you have to be alert constantly, run for the ball often and quickly, and do lots of high jumps. Can you do that for very long?

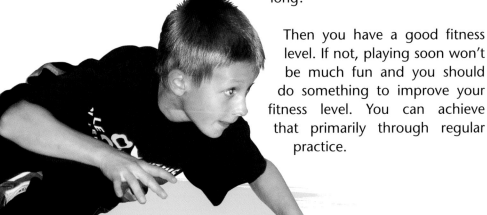

Then you have a good fitness level. If not, playing soon won't be much fun and you should do something to improve your fitness level. You can achieve that primarily through regular practice.

What you should be training for

If you want to be able to jump high, you will need strong muscles in your legs. Strength in your arms, hands, and fingers is important so you can receive the ball securely and continue to play quickly.

In addition it is important for a volleyball player to be able to go after the ball quickly and jump high. For that you need speed and power.

Good flexibility is very important for quick and subtle movements, stretching and diving for the ball.

You need good endurance to handle physical strain for an extended period of time. You won't get winded as quickly when you run, jump, ride a bike or swim. And when it does get strenuous you will soon recover and feel fit again.

In training you won't just hold the ball in your hand and play it over the net. Your coach will certainly have you play many other ball games, gymnastic exercises, and calisthenics, and much more. Join in because all of it helps to make you more fit!

THIS IS HOW YOU CAN PRACTICE

Get moving!

- Jogging
- Biking
- Skateboarding
- Swimming
- Playing basketball
- Playing soccer
- Skiing
- Hiking

... and much more.

Increasing power

- **High jumps**
  You crouch down low and jump up as high as you can. Use a piece of tape, or hold a piece of chalk in your hand to mark the height of your jump on the wall.
  Can you go higher next time?

- **Long jumps**
  Mark a starting line and from a standing position jump as far as you can. Can you jump farther on your next attempts? Who can jump the farthest?

Balance and dexterity

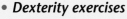

- **Balancing**
Balance on a chalk line or a beam.
You can find low walls in your neighborhood and fallen trees in the forest to balance on.

- **Dexterity exercises**
Many athletic exercises require a sense of balance and dexterity. Try it with inline skating, ice skating, walking on stilts, or riding a mountain bike or a unicycle. Have you ever juggled?

**Which other sports do you enjoy aside from volleyball?
Write them down here.**

_____

_____

_____

. . . . 5 VOLLEYBALL EQUIPMENT

WELL, LUCY! ARE WE PLAYING IN THE GYM OR ON THE BEACH?

A beginning volleyball player also wants to look like a true volleyball player. But what is required? A jersey, of course, in the team colors with your name and number on the back. Add to that matching shorts and socks.

All of that looks great but really isn't necessary in the beginning. You can wear anything to play volleyball. It should be comfortable and not interfere with your playing. In the gym it is important to have proper athletic shoes with non-skid soles. They should give you support when jumping and running. The kneepads protect you from getting bruises and contusions when diving. If you are in a club the teams wear team uniforms for their games.

 *You think there are a lot of volleyballs here? But that's not the case. Only one volleyball has a complete outline. Color it when you find it!*

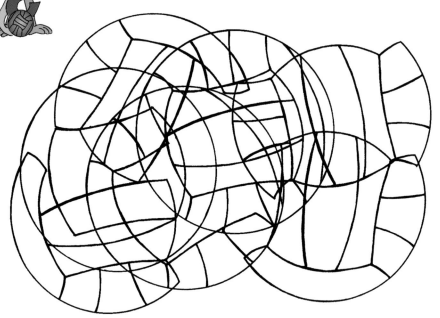

Only two of the volleyballs are identical. Can you find them?

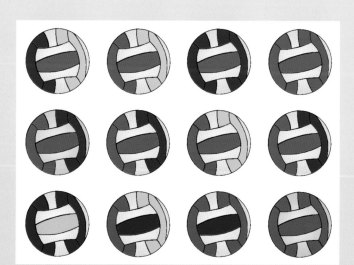

THE BALL

Maybe you have played back and forth over the net with a rubber ball, a softball, an inflatable ball, or even a balloon. It's fun and there are many useful exercises. But soon you should start to play with a real volleyball.

It has a leather or synthetic cover and comes in plain white, in just one light color, or in combinations of colors. The volleyball has a circumference of approximately 26 inches and weighs 9 to 10 ounces.

In international competitions the weight, size, color, the imprint and the manufacturer are specified. All balls used in a match must be identical and approved for the tournament. The referee monitors this.

Do your parents or grandparents always ask you what you would like for your birthday or for Christmas? Next time ask for a volleyball to practice with.

THE CLOTHES

Indoor volleyball

Jersey and shorts

The players wear comfortable shorts and a short – or long – sleeved jersey. At tournaments, all members of the team wear uniforms with numbers.

Kneepads

They are not mandatory as per the regulations, but they are recommended for every player. You protect your knees and thus are less afraid to dive for a ball.

Ankle braces

Some athletes wear this type of protection because all that jumping puts much strain on the ankles. The braces prevent ankle sprains.

Athletic shoes

Your shoes should fit well, provide good support for quick strides and jumps, and should have skid-proof soles.

Beach volleyball

Sun protection

Beach volleyball is played almost exclusively outdoors and ideally in bright sunshine. Therefore you need to really protect yourself with sunscreen.

Headgear

Wear a peaked cap or tie a scarf around your head. Not only does it look cool, but it also protects you from dangerous sunstroke.

Sunglasses

Your eyes need protection from the strong UV-rays and from flying sand.

The sunglasses should fit well, be shatterproof, and should not slide down your nose during quick movements.

Pants and top

The beach volleyball players wear short and formfitting shorts and tops. Not only does it look trendy, but the players are also better able to cope with the heat.

Shoes?

There are no shoes. The players play barefoot. This allows them to stand more easily in the soft sand and push off better when jumping.

IS EVERYTHING PACKED?

You are very excited because you are playing an out-of-town game. You have practiced a lot and the team lineup is set.

Now imagine you arrive at the site, you are standing in the locker room, unpacking your gym bag and ... where are your shoes? Your perfectly broken in super jumping shoes are at home – far away! You just plain forgot them! And you can't just borrow shoes from someone else because they would not fit properly.

The fact that you cannot play now isn't just aggravating to you, but also is a big problem for your team.

Of course your parents could help you pack your bag, but every player is responsible for his own complete and proper equipment!

THE CHECKLIST

Many athletes know that sinking feeling of having forgotten something at a critical competition or tournament. That is why it is important to get everything ready in good time. Pack your gym bag the night before so you can rest easy.

A checklist has proven helpful for many athletes. You write down everything you want to bring along. Check off everything you pack. Use a pencil so you can erase the checks before the next time you pack.

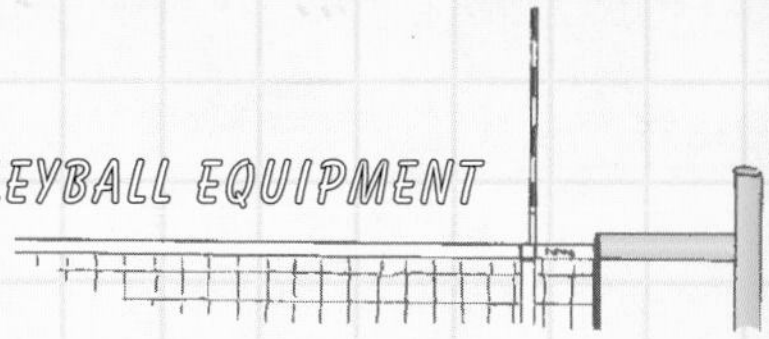

MY CHECKLIST

- ☐ JERSEY

- ☐ SHORTS

- ☐ SOCKS

- ☐ KNEEPADS

- ☐ SHOES

- ☐ TOILETRIES

- ☐ _____

- ☐ _____

- ☐ _____

- ☐ _____

- ☐ _____

- ☐ _____

List anything else you shouldn't forget on the blank lines.

These definitely also belong in your gym bag. Did we forget anything? Then draw it or right it down!

Fruit for a snack.

Water or a juice and water mix for when you're thirsty.

Toiletries for showering.

A hat is very important on cooler days after sweating and showering.

Your good luck charm.

Volleyball players need warm muscles. Therefore, they often wear a warm-up suit before the game and during breaks to keep from getting cold.

A few sweets are sometimes important.

THE COURT

Indoor volleyball

The surface of the court must be level and smooth. Players can easily get caught or twist their ankles on dents and gaps. Make sure that the parquet floor is not damaged. You need to be sure that you won't get splinters in your knees or hands when diving for the ball. Any perspiration on the floor is wiped up so the players won't slip.

Beach volleyball

Beach volleyball is always played on sand. Of course it can really vary. There is loose and deep, and moist and firmly packed-down sand. Also, most of the time the subsurface is not consistent on the entire court. Beach volleyball players prefer to play on a sandy beach.

OH BOY!
I THINK THIS SAND IS A LITTLE TOO DEEP FOR PLAYING!

THE OFFICIAL INDOOR VOLLEYBALL COURT

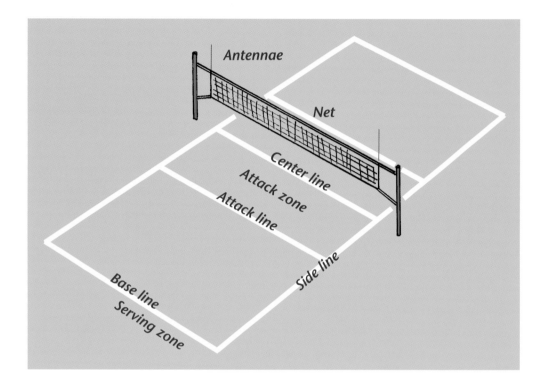

Court size and net height

The height of the net varies according to age and division:

Age 12 and under	Net: 200 cm	(6'5")
Age 14 and under	Net: 212 cm	(6'9")
Age 16 and under	Net: 215 cm	(7'0)

The court measures 9 x 19 m (29'6" x 59'). For women the height of the net is 2.24 m (7'3") and for men 2.43 m (7'9").

The **antennae** have a height of 80 cm (2.6') above the edge of the net. The red and white strips alternate and are always 10 cm wide (3.2").

THE OFFICIAL BEACH VOLLEYBALL COURT

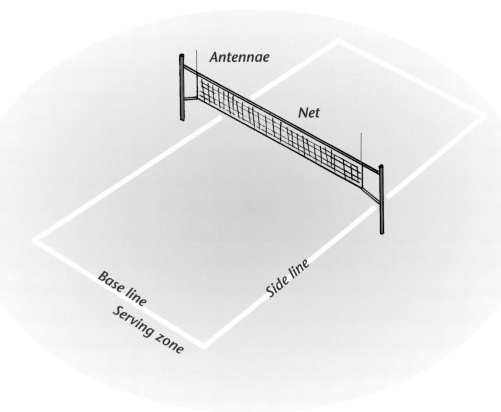

Antennae

Net

Base line

Serving zone

Side line

The court

The court measures **8 x 16 m (26'2" x 52'4")**. Since there are only two players, both can attack and block. That is why beach volleyball does not have an attack line or an attack zone.

Of course it isn't possible to paint colored lines on the sand. Therefore the side lines, the base lines, and the center line are marked by plastic or rubber bands.

The net set-up is the same as in indoor volleyball.

B	A	L	L
	A		
	A		
T	A	N	K
	A		
	A		
P	A	R	K

How do you get from the BALL via the TANK to the PARK?

You can only change one letter in each line to get a new word.

Only one ball makes it over the net. Find out which number it is!

54

.....6 A FEEL FOR THE BALL

What exactly is a feel for the ball?

Is it the joy the ball feels when he sails high and fast through the air?

YAAHOO!

OUCH! OH, OUCH!

Is it the pain it feels after a hard serve or a spike?

OH, MY DEAR BALL!
I JUST LOVE YOU SO MUCH!
I APOLOGIZE FOR ALWAYS HAVING TO
HIT YOU SO HARD!

Or is it the feelings the volleyball player has for the ball?

55

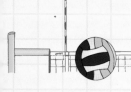

MY VOLLEYBALL

A BALL, SO ROUND, SO BRIGHT, SO FAIR
THE PLAYERS SEND IT THROUGH THE AIR.

THEY DIG, THEY SET, THEY SPIKE, THEY VOLLEY
THE BALL IS LAUGHING, FEELING JOLLY.

AT FIRST I THOUGHT I CAN'T, YOU SEE
HIT THE ONE I LOVE, NOT ME!

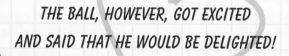

THE BALL, HOWEVER, GOT EXCITED
AND SAID THAT HE WOULD BE DELIGHTED!

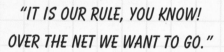

"IT IS OUR RULE, YOU KNOW!
OVER THE NET WE WANT TO GO."

Have you ever tried to write a poem? It is lots of fun.
Just try it and add a few lines to ours.

A feel for the ball refers to how well a player can handle the ball. With his hand and his arm he feels the weight of the ball, its size and the material it is made of. He also feels how it flies and bounces. A good volleyball player must have this feel.

For that you must:

- *Receive the ball with your fingers, hands or forearms.*
- *Pass the ball easily, skillfully and accurately.*
- *Send the ball well aimed and hard into the opposing court.*

In a game, you control the ball. You receive the opponent's serve or your teammate's pass and continue the play. You either make a good pass to your teammate or you make a well-aimed play over the net. You are the boss and you show the ball how it's going to be! The ball isn't the boss of you!

You have to react quickly. In volleyball the player is not allowed to catch the ball or hold on to it while he thinks about how to continue. He has to make quick decisions and react fast as lightning.

That only works with a good feel for the ball. You acquire this feel for the ball only by practicing lots and lots. Even the best volleyball players continue to practice with the ball. It would be best if you took a little time every day. You will find exercises on the following pages. Have fun!

Here the players are practicing in the practice gym.
But surely you can also find a suitable wall at home.

EXERCISES FOR THE FEEL FOR THE BALL

How can you practice?

Standing up, sitting on the floor or sitting on a chair. Take a ball and play with it.

Where can you practice?

You don't need much space for the exercises. You can practice at the park, out in your yard, and even inside as long as it doesn't disturb anyone. You just have to be careful that nothing is broken.

What can you practice with?

The volleyball is your implement. With it you should practice the feel for the ball as much as possible. But any other balls are suitable if an actual volleyball is not available. Use large and small, soft and hard balls.

How fast do you have to practice?

Of course a player should be able to handle the ball very nimbly. But that doesn't happen right away. You do the exercises slowly at first and then try to do them a little faster each time. Later on it has to happen accurately and quickly!

I DON'T HAVE TO FORGO MY EXERCISES EVEN WHEN WATCHING TV.

EXERCISES FOR THE FEEL FOR THE BALL

 Rolling the ball

- Roll the ball on the floor from your right hand to your left hand.
- Use a stone, a bowling pin, a chalk mark, or something similar to mark a goal on the floor and roll the ball to it. How close do you get to the goal? Whose ball gets closest?

- Roll the ball around both feet.
- Roll the ball between your legs in a figure eight pattern.

 Throwing the ball

- Throw the ball from one hand to the other.
- Throw the ball in the air and catch it. Before you catch it turn around and clap your hands, or catch it behind your back.
- Throw two balls at the same time and catch them both.
- While one ball is being thrown in the air the other one is bounced on the floor. That is a pretty difficult task!

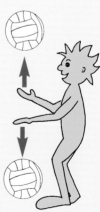

Juggling the ball

- Place the ball on your closed forearms and walk around a marker and back again. Turn it into a competition. Who is fastest?
- Can you do it only on the left or the right forearm?
- Bounce the ball on your forearms. How many repetitions can you do?
- Bounce the ball from one forearm to the other.

Write your record in this little box. Use a pencil so you can always erase the number and write down you new record.

The super-trick

Finally we have a pretty challenging exercise with which you will be able to amaze your friends and family.

Lay the ball down in front of you, then hit the still ball hard with the flat of your hand. You have to pull your hand away very quickly so the ball can bounce up. Now you can bounce the ball.

Practice makes perfect!

When you have tried an exercise and practiced it a few times, you can color the corresponding ball.

You will progress fastest if you practice a lot. Just write down how many times a week you practice.

Write the week in the upper row and then make a line underneath every time you practiced.

WEEK	1.	2.								
NUMBER	ͰͰͰ /									

OH BOY!
I THINK I GOT SOMETHING
MIXED UP HERE!

. . . . 7 PASSING, DIGGING, SERVING

POINT! SET! GAME!

What could be better in volleyball than to skillfully play the ball into the opposing court so no opposing player can reach it, and scoring a point for your team! Sometimes you do this with a little dink or with an unreachable smash. Even the serve is a guaranteed point with some players. The spectators are delighted!

Or maybe you will exasperate the other team when you hit every ball easily and smoothly no matter how hard it is, and handily pass it to a teammate.

All of these successful actions are the result of diligent training. For every play situation there are specific techniques that need to be practiced again and again. For that it is important that you're familiar with the correct posture, the position of feet, hands and fingers, and that you know how the movement progresses.

On the following pages we have illustrated the most important actions in volleyball.

THE MOST IMPORTANT ACTIONS IN VOLLEYBALL

Attacking

Receiving

Passing

Blocking

Back Row

Defense
Serving

WHAT TECHNIQUE DOES A VOLLEYBALL PLAYER REQUIRE?

In order for the game to be fun, even a beginning volleyball player must be able to master a few basic play situations.

Those include:

Receiving the ball.

Passing the ball.

Executing the task.

In this book we describe the initial techniques for this. We show you what the technique looks like, what you have to pay attention to, how you can practice, and which mistakes can crop up during execution.

You will learn best when your coach or an experienced volleyball player demonstrates the technique and you can practice as a group. But when you are at home, you can review the pictures and descriptions in the book at your leisure. Many of the exercises you can do alone, or with your parents, siblings or friends. Always make sure that you're not practicing mistakes. The pictures of mistakes will help you identify these.

PASSING

Passing is also referred to as passing with finger action or setting.

This technique allows you to receive and pass high balls.

This is how you make an overhand pass:

- You are in starting position.

- You have a stable stance.

- Your knees are slightly bent.

- Concentrate on the ball.

- Move toward the ball.

- Lift your arms.

- Go into stride position.

- Bring your hands together in overhand pass position.

- Bend the knees a little more.

- Bend the arms slightly.

- Spread your fingers.

- The fingers assume a "basket" position.

- The thumbs point toward the eyes.

- You see the ball through the "basket."

- The body stretches toward the ball.

- The ball is played overhead directly in front of the forehead.

- The forward pointing area of all ten fingers touches the ball.

- You play the ball with a brief, smooth motion.

- The wrists are heavily bent.

- The thumbs help a lot with passing.

- After passing, the body stretches out after the ball.

- After passing, you are immediately ready for the next play.

Like a basket

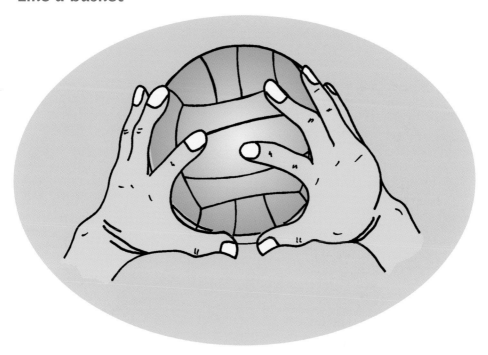

The correct hand position is very important so the ball does not slide out between your fingers. The fingers span the ball and briefly hold it like a basket.

I FEEL TOTALLY SAFE IN A BASKET LIKE THIS ONE.

THIS IS HOW YOU CAN PRACTICE

Here are a few exercises for practicing passing.

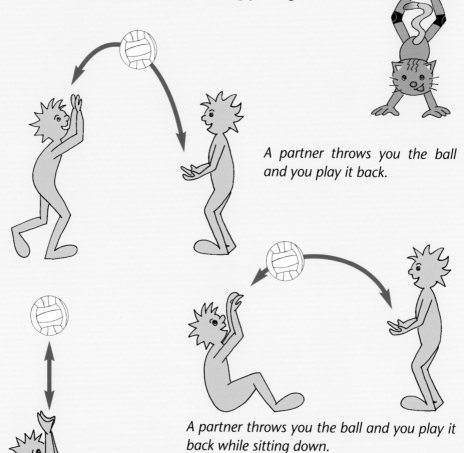

A partner throws you the ball and you play it back.

A partner throws you the ball and you play it back while sitting down.

Set the ball up in the air. Who can do five, ten, or more repetitions? Write your record in the little box, but use a pencil so you can always erase the old record and write in a better result.

Throw the ball into the air

- Pass it to your partner.
- Set the ball once and then catch it.

Play against a wall

- How many repetitions can you do?
- If the ball returns awkwardly after it bounces, set it overhead first and then play it against the wall.

Play against a wall with a partner

- Who can do the most repetitions?
- Who makes the first mistake?

Alternate playing against the wall with only one ball

- How many repetitions can you do together?
- Who makes the first mistake?

When you have tried an exercise and practiced it a few times, you can color the corresponding ball.

These players are making mistakes passing. Can you identify them?

1

2

3

4

Mark the mistake that is also your problem with a check. But, of course, use a pencil so you can soon erase it again.

PLAYING WITH DIRECTIONAL CHANGES

As you know, in a real volleyball game you rarely just play straight back and forth. Most of the time the ball is received from one direction and passed into another direction. That is why you also have to practice these directional changes.

Alone in the corner

If you are alone, look for a corner where you can play against two different walls. First play to the wall on the left, then receive the rebounding ball and play it against the wall on the right. If you can't manage the directional changes right away you can first do an in-between play with the rebounding ball. Use passing and digging.

Make sure that you always have the correct leg forward.

DIGGING

Digging allows you to receive a low ball and pass it. It is a good way to receive a hard hit and then pass it softly to a teammate.

This is how the forward dig is executed:

- You are in starting position.

- Your weight is on the balls of your feet.

- Knees and hips are bent.

- Arms are bent in front of the body.

- You move toward the ball.

- Bring your arms together.

- Put your hands together.

- Bend your wrists downward.

- Extend your arms.

- Hands and forearms are very close together.

- Lower the torso.

- Once again, you have a stable stance in stride-straddle position.

- The knees are straightened somewhat.

- The hands are bent downward.

- The ball is played with the forearms.

- Upon contact with the ball, the arms and shoulders are gently "pushed" forward and up.

- After the pass, the body continues to stretch upward.

- Then immediately be ready to continue playing.

Hand position

- One hand lays in the other.

- The wrists are firmly pressed together.

- The hands bend downward at the wrists.

The hands must come together quickly. Try out which of your hands is better on the top and which is better on the bottom. Keep practicing bringing you hands together quickly and placing one hand in the other.

Arm position

- The forearms are firmly pressed together.

- The elbows are hyperextended.

- The arms are rigid and slightly rotated to the outside and form a rectangle.

- The muscles in the forearms are flexed by the bending of the wrists.

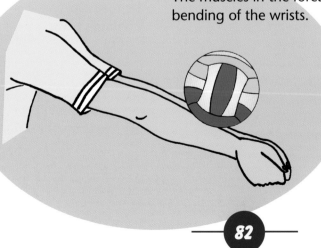

Volleyball players say that the forearms have to be like a board on which the ball is being played. You achieve this extreme tension by pressing your forearms together and rotating them out and by bending your hands downward. Try it!

Always keep your eye on the ball and watch where the ball is going. Move toward the ball and always position yourself so you can receive the ball from the front and then pass it.

Have you ever noticed the stance policemen are in when they point a pistol at a criminal or provide backup? It is the same stable position the volleyball player often assumes when digging.

THIS IS HOW YOU CAN PRACTICE

Here are some exercises to practice digging.

A partner throws you the ball, and you return it with a dig.

A partner throws you the ball, and you return it with a dig sitting down.

Play the ball straight up. Who can do five or ten consecutive repetitions, or more? Write your record in the little box. But use a pencil so you can always erase the old result and write in a better result.

Throw the ball up
- *Dig the ball up once and then catch it.*
- *Dig the ball to a partner.*

Play against a wall
- *How many repetitions can you do?*
- *Mark a point at the wall.*
- *Increase the distance.*

With a partner alternate digging the ball against a wall
- *How many repetitions can you do together?*
- *Who makes the first mistake?*

When you have tried an exercise and practiced it a few times, you can color the corresponding ball.

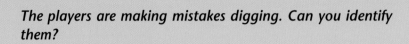
The players are making mistakes digging. Can you identify them?

1

2

3

4

Mark the mistake that is also your problem with a check.
But, of course, use a pencil so you can soon erase it.

A volleyball player must be good at judging which direction and at what trajectory the ball will travel, and also how quickly and how hard it will arrive. You will learn this in many, many training sessions and games.

All of the balls are traveling in the direction of the arrows. Which balls will hit the red target below and which ones will miss?

To solve this problem you can use a ruler and extend the arrows. But try to visualize it first.

THE UNDERHAND SERVE

The serve is important because it brings the ball into play and opens up a move.

With the serve, the player hits the ball over the net, hopefully so skillfully that the opposing team has trouble reaching and returning it.

In doing so, the serving player has to be careful to hit the ball into the opposing court without touching the net or hitting out of bounds.

This task can also be executed from above, overhead. But that is more complicated, which is why in this learning book we have chosen the underhand execution.

This is how the underhand serve is executed:

- Concentrate on the serve.
- The body faces the net.
- Go into stride position.
- If you are right-handed, your left foot should be forward (left-handers should have the right foot forward).

- Swing the right arm far back.
- Knees and hips are bent.
- The weight is on the rear foot.

- At the same time, the ball is thrown up with a smooth motion.
- The hand stays on the ball as long as possible.

- When throwing the ball up, the left arm is nearly extended.

- The serving arm swings back.

- The ball is struck from below with an arched, rigid hand.

- Allow the serving arm to complete the swing.

- Run onto the court and immediately be ready to play.

This girl is performing an underhand serve.

Here she is performing an overhand serve. That is a bit more difficult.

Like the pendulum on a clock

Imagine your arm moves like a clock pendulum. A clock pendulum is rigid and moves straight back and forth. It doesn't swerve, and it doesn't make zigzag movements.

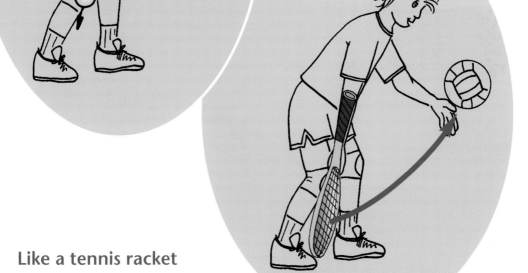

Like a tennis racket

Imagine your forearm and your hand are like a tennis racket. The forearm is the handle and the hand is the striking surface. Have you ever seen the handle and the racket have a wobbly, soft connection or even bend?

THIS IS HOW YOU CAN PRACTICE

For a good and reliable serve, you have to practice a lot. Here we have put together a few exercises for you. You can practice alone or with friends.

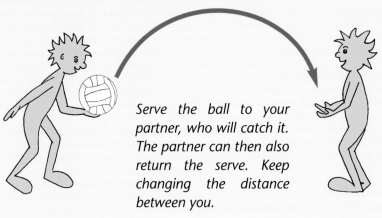

Serve the ball to your partner, who will catch it. The partner can then also return the serve. Keep changing the distance between you.

Serve the ball against a wall and then catch it. You can alternate catching the ball with a practice partner.

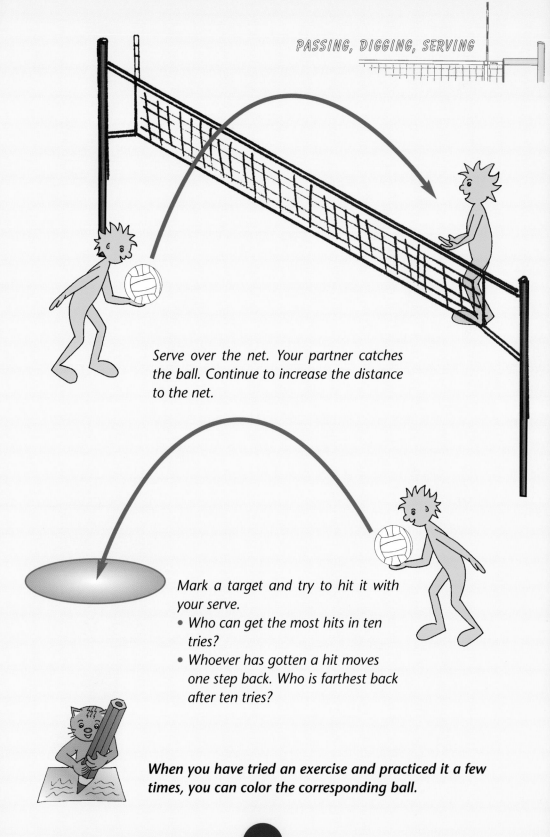

Serve over the net. Your partner catches the ball. Continue to increase the distance to the net.

Mark a target and try to hit it with your serve.
- Who can get the most hits in ten tries?
- Whoever has gotten a hit moves one step back. Who is farthest back after ten tries?

When you have tried an exercise and practiced it a few times, you can color the corresponding ball.

The players are making mistakes serving underhand. Can you identify them?

1

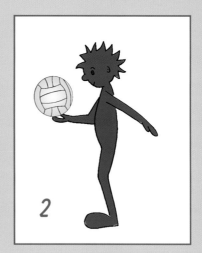

2

3

4

5

6

7

Mark the mistake that is also your problem with a check.
But, of course, use a pencil so you can soon erase it.

Do you like to draw? Who is playing whom here?
Complete this picture!

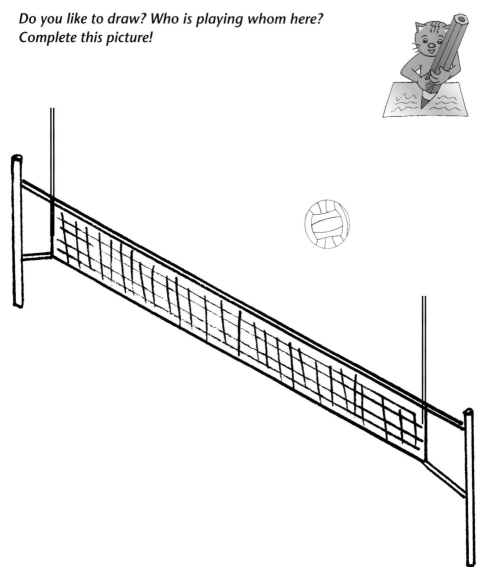

. . . . 8 KEEPING THINGS STRAIGHT

Almost everything in people's lives is regulated. What a mess it would be if everyone could just do whatever they wanted. Families have rules that everyone has to abide by, as do schools, day care, and sports teams. There are traffic rules for road traffic, and every card game has rules.

It is the same in sports. Every sport has rules on how the sport is practiced, how a competition proceeds, and when a team wins or loses. What is allowed and what is prohibited is also regulated.

In volleyball, there is an entire book of rules.
And it's a good thing there are all those rules! Otherwise there would be a lengthy discussion about points and penalties after every action and no one would enjoy the game.

We don't want to write about all of the volleyball rules here. That would be too difficult and not that important for you right now. When you play with friends, you can make your own rules, and at the club the coach will explain everything.

If you are interested, you can read up on all of the volleyball rules online at www.usavolleyball.org.

THE OFFICIAL RULES

In your free time, you can of course play by your own rules. Most important is that everyone playing is in agreement and that everyone accepts the rules and abides by them.

Nevertheless it is very important to know the official volleyball rules and regulations. You can derive your "recreational" rules from there.

The teams

The best thing about volleyball is that it is a team sport. You play together with other athletes; you fight together, rejoice over your victories and are never alone in defeat.

Indoor volleyball

In men's and women's indoor volleyball, there are always six players on a team. That means three players in the front and three players in the back. Good teams even have a libero. But he can only play in the back.

Boys and girls can play on coed teams until age 12.

Beach volleyball

In beach volleyball, teams are made up of two players. There are no substitutes.

Court and net

Whether they are club league games, national league games, the World Championships or even the Olympics, the courts are always the same size and the nets the same height.

- An indoor volleyball court measures **9 x 18 m (59 x 29.6)**.
- A beach volleyball court measures **8 x 16 m (26.2 x 52.4)**.
- The women's net is **2.24 m high (7'3")**.
- The men's net is **2.43 m high (7'9")**.

Children aren't as tall as adults so they are not able to jump as high. Therefore, the nets are a little lower, depending on age. For children under the age of 12, the net is only *2.00 m (6'5")* high.

The ball out of bounds

The team's goal is for the ball to land on the floor of the opposing court. In doing so, you have to be careful that the ball doesn't touch the floor outside of the court. That would mean a point and a serve for the other team. If the ball lands right on the line, it is still on the court.

A player is allowed to run out of bounds to save a ball.

The scope of the ball

In volleyball, the ball can only be played over the net in a certain area. That is called the area of play. We have colored that area yellow. All balls that go over the net in other places or even underneath it are errors.

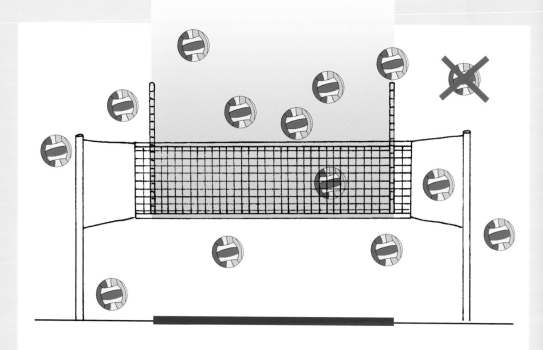

Which balls are played outside of the area of play and are therefore errors? Cross out the "wrong" balls like we've already done with one of the balls.

THE REFEREE

It is important that judges umpire and monitor a real volleyball game where points, victory or defeat are at stake. The referee calls the shots and all players must accept his decisions. That is the case even if you viewed the game situation differently and would make a different call yourself.

When the spectators are cheering and shouting encouragement, it is often very noisy in the gym and the players can hardly hear what the referee is saying. In addition, communication with teams from different countries with different languages is quite difficult. That is why there are international hand signals every player recognizes. Here are a few of the referee's signals.

Service

Four touches on the ball

End of set or game

Time out – break

The ball is out of bounds

Take a close look at the players. What is not consistent with the rules? What are they doing wrong?

ONE, TWO, THREE — WHERE SHOULD I PLAY THE BALL TO NOW?

1

2

SILLY REFEREE! I'M GOING TO DO WHAT I WANT!

3

Do you know any other rule violations? List them here!

_____

_____

_____

FAIRNESS COMES FIRST

Be fair toward your opponent.

You cannot play proper volleyball without an athletic opponent.
Or do you want to always play against a wall?
That is why you need to behave considerately and fairly
toward your opponent.
The athletic opponent is your playing partner.

Be fair toward your teammates.

Everyone does his best and no one makes mistakes intentionally.
Shouting at someone and insulting him serves no purpose.
Instead, help the weaker player so he soon will be able
to better support the team.
Try to "iron out" his mistakes.

Be honest

Be honest with yourself.
When you can't reach a ball, play out of bounds,
or something doesn't work out the way you would like,
don't blame others but rather look to yourself for the mistake first.
Obey the rules, even when the referee isn't looking.

Playing sports together, practicing, preparing for a game, and fighting for victory with your team – that's the best! In doing so, you learn to value friendship, cooperation and camaraderie. Good athletes play fair!

. . . . *9 LET'S PLAY*

To play volleyball in the yard, on the street, at the beach or elsewhere, you don't necessarily need two teams with six players each, a net at the official height, or a court with correct lines. Volleyball is also very fun on a smaller court without lines, over a stretched cord or without any "net" at all. Besides, the various playing opportunities allow you to practice your receiving and passing technique, as well as the walk over.

Find a place that is suitable for playing. Make sure that there is no danger to windows or flowerbeds from stray balls. Avoid freshly painted surfaces and don't go on a heavily traveled street. Got it? Have fun!

PLAYING WITH FRIENDS

Forming teams

You want to form teams but can't agree on players? The two smallest players face each other. You walk toward each other with "coffee beans" – small steps in which the heel of one foot is set against the toe of the other foot. The first one to step on the other's foot gets to pick the first player for his team. Now you take turns choosing until all players have been picked.

The rules

Even if you and your friends are just playing in the park or the school yard, some things do have to be discussed. Lay down your own rules before the game begins.

 Who plays together on a team?

 Where is the "net"?

 Is there an "out of bounds" or do you just keep on playing?

 Is there a base line?

Sometimes you only notice during the game that something remains unsettled.

To avoid disagreements, you can designate one player as the referee.

If no coach, trainer or teacher is present, the players themselves determine the rules. Everyone has a voice! How to play is not decided by the biggest, the strongest, or the one who owns the ball.

Some tips from Felix:

 Make sure you don't disturb anyone!

 Be careful not to break any windows or damage cars or landscaping!

 Watch out for small children or people walking!

 Be aware of newly constructed walls and fresh paint.

 Caution on roads with traffic!

THROWING AND CATCHING

Someone who can throw and catch well and is quick going after the ball has the best qualifications to be a good player.

1 With two players

- *Throw the ball back and forth so the other player can catch it.*
- *Alternate throwing with the right and the left hand.*
- *Catch with both hands, and later with only one hand.*
- *Sometimes throw the ball inaccurately on purpose.*
  Later, don't throw the ball directly to your partner deliberately so he has to chase the ball.

2 With three players

- *You play in a triangle. First play clockwise, and then counter clockwise.*
- *At first, play so the ball is easy to catch. Later make it a little more difficult.*
- *Who drops the ball first?*

Ball over the cord

- *Form two teams and throw the ball over a stretched cord. The ball must be caught and cannot touch the ground. Throw the ball back immediately or play it to a teammate first, who will then play it over the cord.*

Turn it into a competition:

- *Every ball that touches down on the opposing team's side of the court is counted as a point. Which team is first to reach 10 (or even 20) points?*

Most of the time, the ball will not fall right into your arms. That means that you have to quickly determine where the ball is going and then swiftly run to the ball. The faster you are in the right position, the more time you have to get ready to catch.

Monkey in the middle

Two players face each other and throw the ball back and forth. The third player stands in the middle and tries to catch the ball. When he catches it, he trades places with the player who made the mistake.

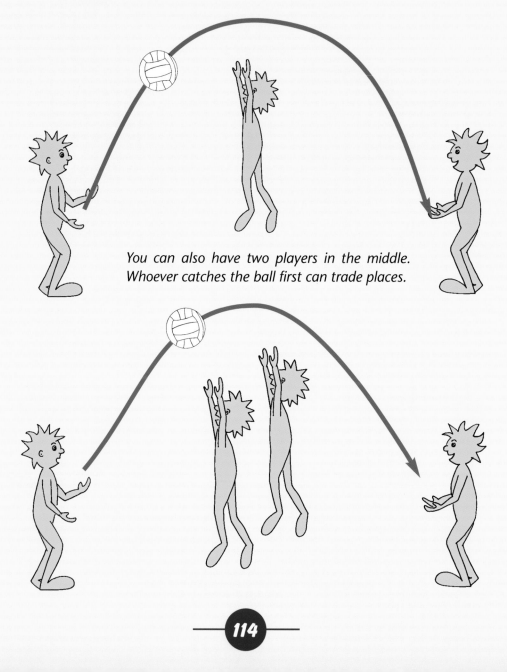

You can also have two players in the middle. Whoever catches the ball first can trade places.

PASSING AND DIGGING

Of course, in a real volleyball game you don't just pass and dig but you use and adapt all techniques, depending on the game situation. Let's practice that now!

 ## Two on one

You stand opposite the other two players and play the ball to one of them. You get the ball back from him and then play it to the second player. If your opposing players stand close together, the directional change won't be too great for you. But if they move farther apart, it will become more difficult.

Now make it more difficult for your opponents. Occasionally play back to the same player again. Does he react quickly enough?

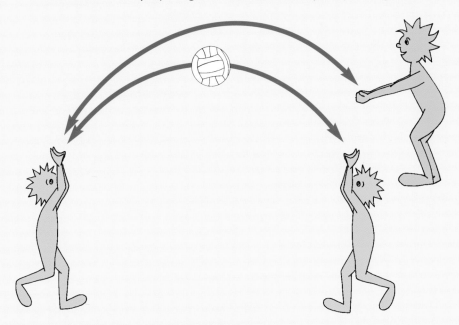

You can also do this exercise with two balls.

2 Three in a triangle

Three players form a triangle and play the ball to each other.

- **This makes it a little easier:**
  If you can't manage the change of direction to the other player right away, play the ball straight up first and then pass it on.

- **1. Difficulty:**
  Change directions – counter clockwise and then clockwise.

- **2. Difficulty:**
  Each time before you pass the ball, play it straight up while spinning around once.

- **3. Difficulty**
  Clap your hands once (or even twice) each time before you receive the ball.

- **All exercises can also be performed with four or five players!**

- **Make sure that the outside leg is always forward!**

Three in a row

Two players stand opposite each other. The third player stands in the middle. Now there are many playing alternatives as you can see from the drawing.

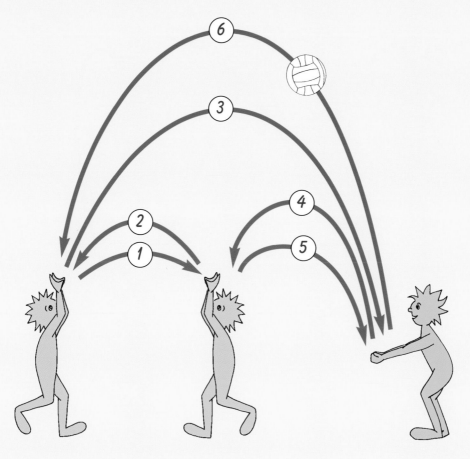

Of course, whoever is in the middle always has to turn to the ball.

Playing with four

The arrows in the drawing show how many possibilities there are when two sets of two players stand opposite each other.

Pay attention!

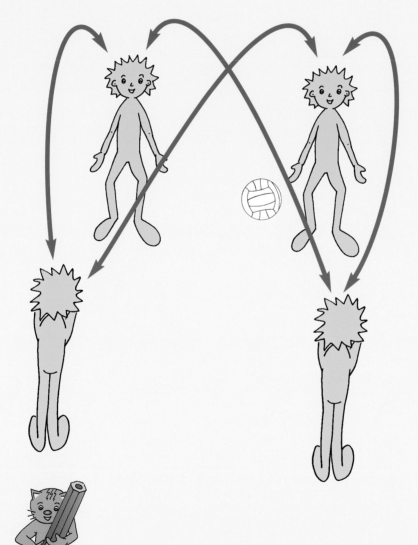

When you have tried an exercise and have practiced it a few times, you can color the corresponding ball.

 ## Ball over the net and chasing after it

Any number of players (but a minimum of three) stands opposite each other in two groups. The court is divided by a net or a cord.

The front player always hits or digs the ball over the net and then runs under the net to the other side. There he gets back in line. When he gets to the front again he plays the ball and runs back under the net to the other side (always going to the right).

When you have tried an exercise and practiced it a few times, you can color the corresponding ball.

.... 10 FIT AND HEALTHY

Most people who participate in sports want to have fun and succeed. Aside from that, an important goal is to keep your body fit and healthy.

EATING RIGHT

Someone who participates in sports, runs and jumps, uses up more energy than a couch potato. That is why food always tastes best after those practice sessions – because you are hungry and thirsty and have to replenish your energy supply.

Almost all children like to eat chocolate, chips, French fries, and pizza. But that's not the best food for athletes, particularly if you eat these things too frequently and in large quantities. These foods contain too much fat.

The better meal for an athlete consists of whole grain bread with cheese, fruit and yogurt. There are many foods that are healthy and taste good, too. Try to have a varied and moderate diet.

This athlete is really hungry after practice. He would like to just eat and drink everything at once. What would you recommend? Cross out anything that, in your opinion, is not very healthy!

Which food should you eat more frequently during the day, and when you need a snack? Cross out every L, Y, M, A, X, E, K and D.

F	D	K	A	R	E	X	Y	M	L	A
M	E	L	M	A	U	D	I	K	D	Y
Y	A	D	D	L	K	Y	M	A	M	T

IF YOU SWEAT, YOU HAVE TO DRINK REGULARLY

When you sweat during training and while playing, your gym clothes are often soaked and you can see the perspiration on your skin.

Sweating isn't bad – in fact, it's very healthy. But your body misses the fluids you lose when you sweat. That's when you have to drink a lot so your body has enough fluids once again.

Thirst quenchers

The best thirst quenchers are

- Water

- Mineral water

- Water and juice mix (apple juice, orange juice or cherry juice diluted with water)

- Herbal tea or fruit tea (also sweetened with honey)

Pure juice and soft drinks are not suitable for replenishing fluids. They contain too much sugar.

When you are thirsty and drink, you have to be careful not to drink too hastily. It is better to take smaller sips more often. Swallow. Be careful not to fill your stomach so full that you will barely be able to move.

OH BOY! MY STOMACH IS SO FULL! I JUST HAD A GIANT THIRST!

HELLO, DOCTOR!

"Hello, Doctor," is what you will cheerfully say to your doctor because, as an athlete, you usually feel fit all around. But even if you're not sick, you should see the doctor at least once a year for a checkup. Tell him that you play volleyball. He will examine you and tell you that you can train without concern.

Have your vaccination record checked and get some nutritional tips.

A successful day begins with a good start in the morning!

A few tips from Felix:

Go to bed on time and get plenty of sleep!

Look forward to the new day.

Stretch after getting up. How about some morning calisthenics? On the following page, you will find some exercises.

A cold shower is ideal after washing. It is refreshing and toughens you up.

Whole grain bread, granola, cornflakes, milk, yogurt and fruit are all part of a good and healthy breakfast.

Don't forget to brush your teeth after you eat!

Don't forget to warm up!

Surely your trainer always allows for a warm-up at the beginning of a training session. It is important that your muscles become warm, loose and flexible through different exercises. That is how you protect yourself from injuries.

When you do exercises at home or play with your friends, don't forget to warm up!

WARM-UP EXERCISES

To warm up, you can jog or do some easy jumping exercises.

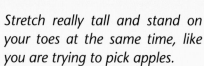

Stretch really tall and stand on your toes at the same time, like you are trying to pick apples.

Now collapse suddenly and make yourself really small.

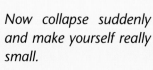

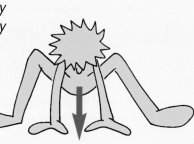

Lie flat on your back and push your pelvis upward.

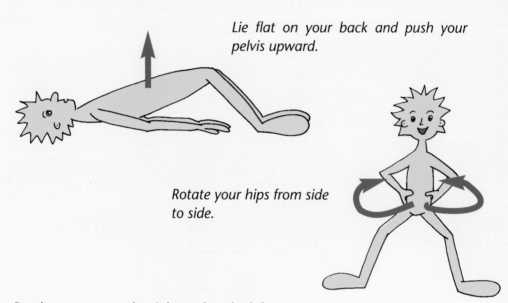

Rotate your hips from side to side.

Bend your torso to the right and to the left.

Do you sometimes have problems getting going in the morning? These exercises are also well suited as morning calisthenics.

Felix is thirsty.

How does he get to his glass?

. . . . . 11 PLAYING FOR A CLUB

At some point, you will find that playing in the backyard, on the street or against a wall behind the house is no longer enough. That's when it is time to join a club. There you can play on a team, be a part of the action and compete in real tournaments.

How do you join a club?

 Find out if your parents will give their approval to your playing volleyball for a club. If yes, find a volleyball or sports club in your community or near your home.

 If you are lucky, your friends or school buddies are already playing on a team and will take you along to their practice.

 Most of the time, sports clubs have an information desk or a bulletin board where telephone numbers or practice times are posted. Make an appointment to try out. Then you can take your time seeing how everything works. You can meet the trainer and the other children and you can see how they practice. Of course, everything is new and strange at first. That's totally normal!

Most of the time you are asked how old you are and which age group you belong in. That is how you are classified for a team in the club. It depends on your birth year and not what grade you are in.

 Now you will try out for a club of your choice or participate in a practice session on a trial basis. Your parents, older siblings or grand parents should accompany you. Bring along gym clothes and athletic shoes.

 If you like it and the trainer says you are suited for playing volleyball, you should sign up. You become a member of the club and receive a membership card.

LOOK! I THINK THAT'S JUST THE THING FOR US!

MY FIRST VOLLEYBALL CLUB

My first club is called: _____

Date of joining: _____

My first trainer: _____

My first team: (names, signatures)

Our team colors: _____

Our logo:

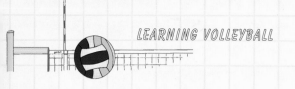

Keeping track of the game results is interesting and fun.

You can record them on this page. If you run out of space, start a game notebook.

Opponent	Result

What does a club and team member have to do?

- Train diligently and perform well in games.
- Pay a monthly membership fee.
- Take care of the club's uniform and clothing.

What does the club have to do?

- Insure the athletes against sport-related accidents and injuries.
- Organize the training and game activities.
- Issue a player's pass to the member.
- Provide the team uniform and possibly launder it.
- Organize transportation to games.
- Provide trainers and coaches at the club.

Can I also leave the club or change over to another club?

- If you want to leave the club or change over to another club, you should cancel your membership in writing.
- There sometimes can be a changeover ban.

Do I always have to go to practice?

- Punctuality and regularity are important rules in sports. Otherwise, you won't learn anything.
- If you really can't make it to a practice session, try to let the trainer or coach know beforehand.
- Schoolwork comes before training.

How can I continue to grow as a volleyball player?

In the interview with Jörg Ahmann, you already read about his progression from playing in Kindergarten to becoming a top player on the national team. If you, too, want to achieve more, your progression might look something like this:

- You participate with your team in the competitive circuit and soon you may move up to a stronger team in a bigger club.
- If you are a good player and a good student, you may be able to attend a school on a volleyball scholarship.
- Soon you will decide if you want to play beach volleyball in addition to indoor volleyball.
- If, at some point in the future, you enjoy helping the younger players practice, you can become an assistant coach.

. . . . *12 VOLLEYBALL GLOSSARY*

Back row defense . . The opposing team's offensive is not blocked but rather parried from the back.

Ball contact . . . . Every player can only touch the ball once briefly (so don't catch or hold the ball). Each team is always allowed to make contact with the ball three times.

Base line . . . . That is the name for the rear boundary line of each half of the court.

Basic line-up. . . . . This refers to the positioning of the six players on the court. There are three front row players and three back row players.

Defense . . . . . Volleyball players differentiate between parrying the serve, blocking, and back row defense. An attack is built on a successful defense.

Digging . . . . This is an underhand defensive or passing technique. The ball is played with the forearms.

Diving . . . . This is a defensive technique for reaching far away balls. To do so, a player has to be gutsy and the technique must be well practiced.

Double contact . . . An error in which one player touches the ball twice in a row.

Error . . . . This happens when a player doesn't receive the ball or doesn't receive it well enough, passes badly, or violates the rules. An error means the opposing team scores a point and wins the serve.

Game point . . . . . The first team to win three sets wins the game. The serve that may bring the final victory is called game point.

Mini volleyball. . . Children have more fun if at first they can play with fewer players on smaller courts with lower nets.

Netball . . . . A ball that touches the edge of the net. It is not an error, but it is very startling and unpredictable for the opposing team.

Offensive . . . . . . The attacker attempts to hit the ball over the net into the opposing court in such a way that the opponent won't be able reach the ball. This is successful primarily through a hard offensive hit, but also through speed and the element of surprise.

Out of bounds . . That means any ball that touches the ground outside of the court or an object.

Pass . . . . The ball is passed on to a teammate and played as an offensive hit. There are long, high, short and wide passes.

Point . . . . Volleyball uses the point system for scoring. A successful move and the associated error by the opposing team, bring in a point.

Position . . . . At the time of the serve, every player has to take a specific position on the court, which he can only leave after the serve has been hit.

Rally . . . . This is what the segment of the game that begins with a serve and ends with an error is called. In doing so, the ball often crosses over the net several times.

Rally point

scoring system . . Every successful move, and thus the opposing team's error brings a point. (In the past, a team had to win the serve to be able to score a point).

Receiving . . . . This refers to the parrying of the serve. In doing so, the ball is most often passed to a teammate.

Service . . . . This is how every move begins. The server stands in the serving zone and hits the ball into the opposing court. The lines are part of the court.

Set ball . . . . This is the serve at the end of a set. The set can be won with this move.

Winning a set . . . . The first team to score 25 points wins the set. But it must be ahead by at least two points.

Here you can write down other terms that are important and that you want to memorize!

· · · · · · · · · · · · · 13 SOLUTIONS

Pg. 10 **In the picture:**
Basketball, volleyball, table tennis, football, hockey, soccer, tennis.

What else we thought of:
Baseball, handball, rhythmic gymnastics, polo, water polo

Pg. 18/19 There are 20 balls on both pages.

Pg. 24

Pg. 44

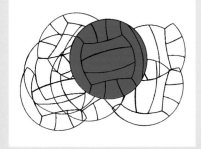

Pg. 54   Ball 4 makes it over the net.

B	A	L	L
T	A	L	L
T	A	L	K
T	A	N	K
B	A	N	K
B	A	R	K
P	A	R	K

Pg. 74/75 Passing errors:

1 No firm stance.
2 The ball is too far back.
3 The eyes are not on the ball but looking downward.
4 The ball is too far away.
5 The fingers are "rolled" into a fist.
6 The player stands too rigid and stiff.
7 The eyes are not on the ball.

Pg. 86/87 Digging errors:

1 The arms are too high.
2 The arms are too low.
3 The ball is not being played with the forearms.
4 The player has a hollow back, is too rigid and stiff.
5 The rear end is "pushed out" – not a proper playing stance.
6 The hands and forearms are open.
7 The eyes are not on the ball.

Pg. 88

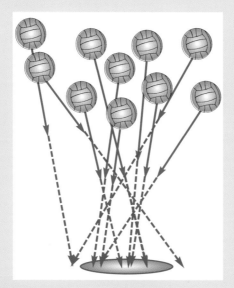

Pg. 96/97 **Serving errors:**

1 The wrong leg is forward.
2 Not in stride position.
3 Not concentrating on the ball.
4 The ball is held too high.
5 The hitting arm is bent.
6 The torso is bent back.
7 The ball is being thrown too far away.

Pg. 102

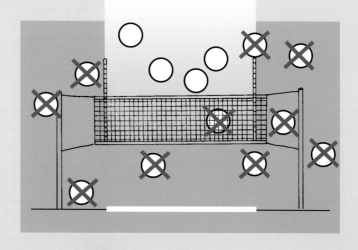

Pg. 104/105 Errors and rule violations:

1 No player may touch the ball twice in a row.
2 The player may not hang on the net.
3 Treat the referee with respect and obey his decisions.
4 The ball should be played, but not caught or held on to.
5 If the ball touches down on one's own side of the court, the opposing team gets the point. By bouncing the ball, you voluntarily give them a point.
6 No player may crawl under the net and enter the playing area of the opposing team.

Pg. 122

F	D	K	A	R	E	X	Y	M	L	A
M	E	L	M	A	U	D	I	K	D	Y
Y	A	D	D	L	K	Y	M	A	M	T

Pg. 128

. . . . 14 LET'S TALK

If this were a book for adults, these pages for the parents and trainers would of course appear at the very front of the book as the preface. But since it is a book for children we are putting this chapter at the end, sort of as an addendum.

Our beginning volleyball players are mostly elementary school students who have just learned to read and have not yet had that much exposure to books. They are absolutely in need of support from big people who can help them with understanding the book.

The best way to start is by leafing through the book and looking at the pictures, and filling in the questionnaire and recording the personal information. This book does not have to be read back to back but is also very useful as a reference work and diary. Have fun reading together!

DEAR VOLLEYBALL PARENTS

Do you remember the first time your little son or daughter chased after a ball and wanted to play with it? Maybe you'll say: As soon as my child was able to walk! Your child never lost this fascination with the ball and has chosen one of the many ball sports. He wants to learn to play volleyball, maybe even practice at a club with experienced coaches and well trained trainers. It is great that you want to support him or her in learning this appealing sport.

Volleyball is an ideal sport for children. The basic idea is simple and the basic skills can be learned quickly. The material requirements are minimal – a ball and a cord. In addition, volleyball distinguishes itself through its great diversity of movement, it is demanding in terms of technique, skill and endurance, and promotes concentration and quick decision-making. Since the teams are separated by a net there is no direct physical contact with the opposing players, and thus less risk of injury. Your child is part of a social community and learns about the particularities of team play, as well as the importance of the individual player. He learns to assert himself and cope with success and failure in playing.

Personal responsibility must be learned, too. By and by, the players take responsibility for the care and completeness of the equipment and pay attention to punctuality and regularity in training and competition. So be supportive of your child's learning to play volleyball, practicing and training. In the beginning the enjoyment of playing, movement, digging and hitting in the various forms of play is prevalent with our little players. Of course, this does require some basic technique, but that should not be the main focus just yet. The children should play, have fun, and in doing so develop their skills.

That is also our wish with this book. Next to the explanations of necessary basic technique and volleyball rules the children also learn a lot about the game of volleyball in general. They have the opportunity to become actively involved in their favorite sport.

Be helpful, but with prudence and patience!

Do not allow your expectations for your child to get too high. What matters most is the enjoyment of the sport and playing. Excessive ambition would only be harmful. Don't compare your child to others of the same age because biological development, particularly at this age, can vary greatly. Just focus on your own child and praise his or her progress. Your child will thank you!

Parental support

Parental support is in demand in volleyball, too. Be it for the purchase of workout clothes, rides to the gym or to games. Surely Mom or Dad, or even Grandma or Grandpa have to be available as partners for playing and practicing.

When your child is part of a team, some of your weekends will be affected by the playing activities. If a game is scheduled for Saturday or Sunday, the family has breakfast by the alarm clock, the parents provide transportation for part of the team, and the siblings want to come

along to cheer. Sunday dinner has to wait until the whistle blows, and visits to Grandma's are only planned for days without games.

But what's better than seeing your own eager little player be irrepressibly happy about winning his first point? Or how much trust and intimacy parents and children experience when a defeat requires comforting?

Be glad that your child is getting regular exercise regardless of whether your child will become an internationally successful super-player or is "only" enjoying the game and the camaraderie.

And one more thing:

Children are unnerved by parents shouting during a game. The children need to make their own decisions, and technical suggestions, as well as substitutions are the trainer's responsibility.

DEAR VOLLEYBALL TRAINER

Surely you'll agree that it is a great feeling to see these little guys with their excited faces and expectant eyes. Now it is up to you to introduce them to volleyball.

But all children are different. There are the self-confident ones and the timid ones, the diligent and the not-so-diligent, the talented and the less talented. Each child has his own little personality with individual qualifications and his own developmental history, with hopes and desires, with feelings and needs. They all have our regard in equal measure.

Children want to be active, to move and have fun. Particularly in a group they are able to match themselves with their peers and spur each other on. A beginning volleyball player's most important role model is his coach or trainer. They watch everything very closely: How he dresses, how he handles the ball, how he speaks to the children, and also how well he adheres to the safety regulations.

The young player himself is the most important factor in the teaching and learning process. The child, no matter how young and how much of a beginner he may be, is always subject to his own development and is never just the object of our influence. Therefore, offer him sufficient tips and opportunities for his own development. Foster and utilize your little beginning volleyball player's independence. Take the path from directing to inspiring.

What a children's volleyball trainer should have:

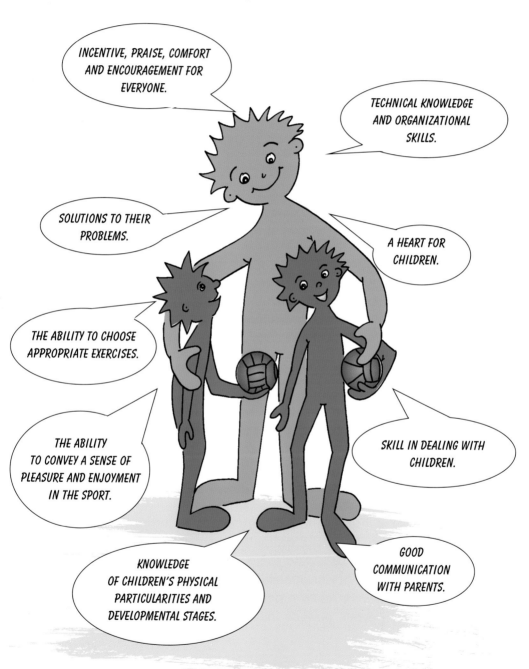

The value of this little book

The value of this little book will depend entirely on how you will integrate it into the instruction. It is written specifically for children who are beginning volleyball players. But it can also be recommended to parents who wish to accompany their child on this path.

The book focuses on the children's needs and is intended to help them engage in volleyball outside of the gym as well. The child acquires a fairly complete foundation for practicing via the book's illustrations and descriptions.

He will be better able to follow your explanations and demonstrations. The young players can review at their leisure what they have learned, keep track of goals and learning progress, and receive suggestions for practicing at home and with other children. This develops the ability to act independently and accelerates the learning process. An environment is created in which the children themselves, step by step, think about their practicing and learning, their movements, actions, and finally monitor and evaluate their behavior.

They become partners of the coaches and trainers. We would like the children to enjoy coming to practice and go home with a sense of achievement. And of course that would make the practice sessions fun for the trainer as well.

The book and training

Tell the children that this book will be their personal companion while they learn to play volleyball. Give them the logo of the club and take a photo to paste in the book. This will boost their attachment to you, the team and the club.

Help the children to use this book properly. In the beginning, read some segments together and explain to the children how the photos

and illustrations should be viewed and understood. Together with the little players make entries regarding goals, suggestions, etc. In doing so, you create critical orientation guides for their understanding and independent practicing.

With the aid of this book you can also assign homework for the next training session. The children read up on a topic and get to do a show-and-tell at the next session.

We always welcome suggestions and additions.

> *We wish you and your little protégées lots of fun and enjoyment,*
> *and of course athletic successes, too.*

PHOTO & ILLUSTRATION CREDITS:

Cover design:	Jens Vogelsang, Aachen
Illustrations:	Katrin Barth
Cover photo:	Fotoagentur Volker Minkus, Isernhagen
	Berndt Barth
Photos (inside):	Jörg Ahmann, Berndt Barth, Thilo von Hagen, Richard Heuchert, Jens Linkerhand

Volleyball for Boys and Girls

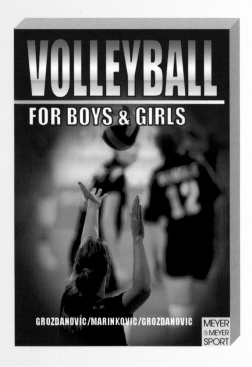

Grozdanovic/Marinkovic/Grozdanovic

168 pages
Full-color print, 9 photos
250 figures and tables
Paperback, 5 $^3/4$" x 8 $^1/4$"
ISBN 1-84126-126-2
£ 12.95 UK/$ 17.95 US
$ 25.95 CDN/€ 16.90

Many years of systematic and complex preparation of young players are necessary in order to prepare them for the physical and psychological efforts, demanded by a high level of training and competition. The youngest age (6-14 years) is the most convenient for learning. This book describes the most suitable training for this age group. It is an ideal introduction to Volleyball for all boys and girls.

MEYER & MEYER SPORT

MEYER & MEYER distribution@m-m-sports.com• www.m-m-sports.com